C000145531

MEMORIES OF MILNTHORPE FOR THE MILLENNIUM

A look back at a Westmorland village before 1950

by

ROGER K. BINGHAM

MEMORIES OF MILNTHORPE

© Roger K. Bingham 2000

ISBN 0 950 9991 1 3

Other books by the same author:

Our Village (1977)

The Church at Heversham (1984)

The Chronicles of Milnthorpe(1987) Cicerone Press

The Lost Resort - The Flow and Ebb of Morecambe (1990) Cicerone Press

Kendal: A Social History (1995) Cicerone Press

From Fell and Field - A History of the Westmorland County Show
1799-1999 (1999) Cicerone Press

CONTENTS

1: Why Milnthorpe?

Milnthorpe is an ancient and historic place.

View from St Anthony's Hill showing 'the clump' on the crest of Dallam Park (left) and St. Anthony's Tower. 'The clump' marks the site of an Iron Age fort dating from c. 200 BC. The hill's name is derived from its having been given as part of the endowment of St. Anthony's Chapel in Kendal Parish Church in c.1500 AD. The Tower, known as 'The Summer House', was built by Henry Smithies of Bela Mill to commemorate the passing of the first Parliamentary Reform Bill in 1832. As such it is possibly unique being the only known monument to the new law, which began the historically important process of extending voting rights for all adults.

BELA MILLS MILNTHORPE

Milnthorpe is 'the place with mill'.

Described, in the 1950's, by the poet Norman Nicholson as 'a place with its sleeves rolled up' Milnthorpe has always had a workaday aspect.

Its name derives from 'Mylna' or 'Millen' 'porp'. If it stems from 'Mylna' Milnthorpe was founded by Danish Vikings who settled here about 850 A.D.; if from 'Millen' the first Milnthorpians were Norse Vikings who arrived a hundred years later. Around 1770 there were eleven water mills stretching along Milnthorpe's river The Bela. Here we see in c1900 cottages on the left once a paper mill with Bela Mills by this time a Comb Mill behind. The millpond in front is known as the 'Clough' and the pathway on the left is part of 'The Strands'.

Milnthorpe is a route centre.

Blount's map of 1826 (left) clearly shows west-east roads leading from the Port of Milnthorpe beyond the mouth of the Bela. The north-south road had recently been constructed by John Macadam. As may be glimpsed from the centre of the map there were not clear cross roads where the roads met but an awkward 'S' bend which was not straightened out until the coming of the motoring era in the 1920's.

The numbers refer to the Poor Law assessment whose rates paid for the upkeep of the Workhouse - top right - close to Milnthorpe's satellite hamlet of Ackenthwaite.

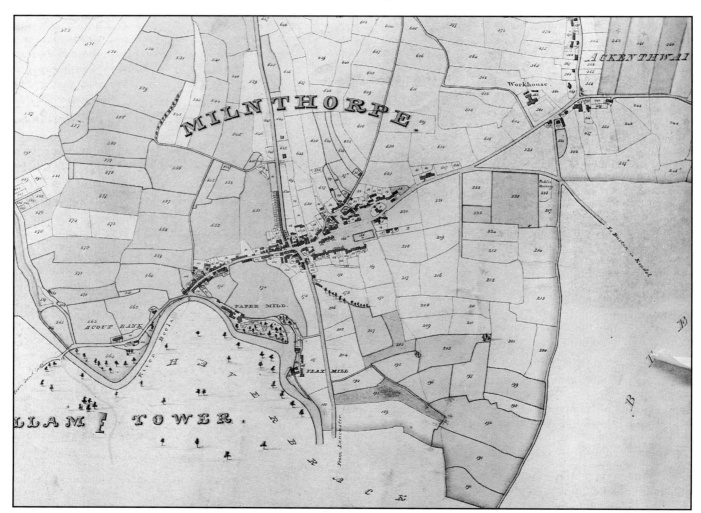

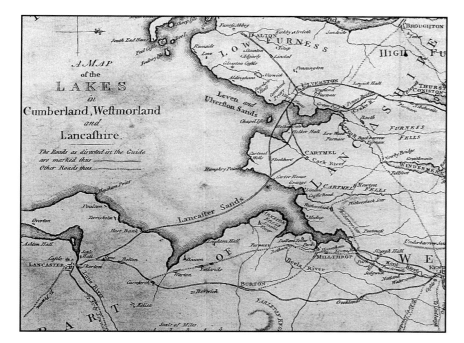

West's Map of 1789

The village is also an 'in between place' as Lands End is 416 miles away and John o' Groats 420. Since 1948 it has been between two National Parks: The Lake District and The Yorkshire Dales.

Most twentieth century travellers associated Milnthorpe with some of the worst snarl ups on the A6 at the village's notorious cross roads before the M6 was opened in 1970. Historically Milnthorpe's main connections with the wider world came via the Kent Estuary half a mile to the west on the final thrust of Morecambe Bay.

West's map shows the cross bay routes and the southeastern road which connected Milnthorpe with old north-south main road at Burton-in-Kendal.

Main Street c.1900.

The historic importance of the link between the estuary and the former main road away to the east is indicated by the name Main Street being given to west-east axis of the village. When this photo was taken the days of the old carrying trade were long over and the bicycle was becoming popular. Even so it was still safe for the village lads to lounge in their Sunday best in the vehicle free highway.

Church Street. c1910.

To the utter confusion of strangers Milnthorpe's Church Street leads not to the village's own Anglican church in the centre of the village but to the former mother church at Heversham over the hill a mile and a half away to the north. There was a joint township of Heversham with Milnthorpe until 1896 when Milnthorpe became a separate civil parish. For religious purposes Milnthorpe remained part of Heversham's ecclesiastical parish until 1924 though the village's own church had been built in 1837. Only in 1999 did Milnthorpe break from Heversham to become an individual ward of South Lakeland District Council.

This **Parish Boundary post** forged by Day's ironmasters of Kendal in 1819 does not mention Milnthorpe because the village was in Heversham Parish. The post is sited at the corner of Burton Road and Paradise Lane at Ackenthwaite.

Paradise Lane probably takes its name from 'para' meaning an edge or boundary and not from the tradition that it was a lovers lane nor because one could 'shoot through Paradise' to Beetham Church which was nearer to part of Ackenthwaite than was its official Parish Church at Heversham.

Milnthorpe was Westmorland's only seaport.

Until the coming of the railways the Port of Milnthorpe had many ships including 'the Eliza', ' the Isobel', 'the Tickler', 'the Thomas' and 'the Dove'. But the most famous Milnthorpe ship was 'the John'. Built about 1760, weighing 52 tons with a single 30foot mast she was used by the Bush family to export gunpowder, hides, wool and grain from Milnthorpe and to bring in all manner of goods from coal, timber, wine, 'red herrings', bricks and tombstones. She was wrecked finally in 1861 off Garston while transporting salt.

'The John of Milnthorp' is depicted here on a teapot to be seen at Abbot Hall, Kendal.

Milnthorpe is a trading centre.

Between 1850 and 1950 there were around 20 shops.
These have diminished in number since the advent of mass motoring so that most 21st century villagers do the bulk of their shopping at out of town centres elsewhere. But other businesses ranging from publishing, vets, IT, to an opticians and beauty parlour have taken the place of grocers and general stores.

Whips' 'Bike Shop'
Park Road c.1910.

Mrs Griffin's Toffee Shop , Main Street 1919. The shop was demolished in 1920 but part of the wall remains.

Chris Knight had a 'Pot Shop' in Park Road in c.1900 but his sign proclaimed him as a 'Grocer and Provisions Dealer, Licensed for Patent Medicines, Tobacco and Snuff'.

Milnthorpe is a centre for much of South Westmorland.

Its market founded by Alexander de Wyndsore in 1334 still flourishes although it lapsed in the mid twentieth century. From the Market Cross, the annual fairs were announced, sinners denounced and monarchs proclaimed as in this photograph of the proclamation of George V in May 1910.

Extract From the Milnthorpe section in
Parson's and White's Directory of 1829 .

HEVERSHAM PARISH DIRECTORY.

2 Hatrop Wm. Birbeck
1 Thompson Anthony
LINEN AND WOOLLEN DRAPERS.
Barrow Richard, (woollen)
Boyd John
Bullman Thomas
Hewetson Henry
MALTSTERS.
Huddleston Thomas
Rawlinson Ewan, St. Anthony's
MANUFACTURERS (LINEN, FLAX, &c.) in *Milnthorp and the Neighbourhood.*
Ashburner John, twine mfr.
Atkinson Thomas, flax spinner and twine manufacturer, Holme
Barker Wm. flax spinner and rope mnfr. Crooklands
Briggs James, twine mfr.
Caton Robert & Son, flax spinners, wrapper & sacking mfr. Cross mill
Cornthwaite Joseph & Co., flax & tow spinners, linen, wrapper & sacking mfr., Halfpenny mill
Greenwood John, wool carder, stocking & blanket yarn mfr. Stainton mill
Hacking Wm. twine mfr., Clawthrop
Jackson Lancelot, linen-manufacturer
Huddlestone Thomas, twine manufacturer
Postlethwaite Wm. bag and sail manufacturer
Smithies Henry & Sons, flax and tow spinners, rope, twine, bed tick, wrappers, & sacking manufacturers, Milnthorpe mills
Waithman & Co. flax spinners and mfrs., Holme mill
MILLINERS & STRAW HAT MAKERS.
*Marked * are Straw Hat Makers.*
Davis Catharine, (and stay maker)
Hudson Jessy
*Inman Ann
Patterson Eliz., New row
*Robinson Mary

PAINTERS & GLAZIERS.
Mills John (and plumber)
Mills William
PAPER MFRS.
Hardy Richard
Turner Wm., Waterhouse
Williamson James
SADDLERS.
Sharpless Joseph
Turner Joseph
SHOPKEEPERS.
Addison John
Briggs Mary (and baker)
Gibson Robert
Spencer John
STONEMASONS.
Brocklebank John
Brocklebank Robert
Brocklebank Thomas
Jackson William
Fleming William
Hudson Robert
SURGEONS.
Jackson William
Mossop Isaac
Parsons William
TAILORS & DRAPERS.
Barrow Richard
Walker Edward
Walker John
Whitaker Thomas
TALLOW CHANDLER.
Armistead Henry (and flour dealer
COACHES.
(*From the Cross Keys.*)
The Telegraph to Lancaster, *via Burton,* at ½ past 9 mng. and to Kendal at 5 evg.; and *via Beetham* to Lancaster at 7 mng., and to Kendal at 6 evg.
A Branch Coach (Telegraph) to Ulverstone, every Sun. Mon. Wed. & Fri. at half-past six evg.; rets. ½ past 9 mng.
(*From the King's Arms.*)
The Fair Trader to Manchester and Liverpool, at 7 mng.; to Kendal at 7 evg.
WATER CARRIAGE.
From the Quay, at Arnside Point, Captain Robert Greenwood's two vessels, trade regularly to Liverpool
From Hest Bank vessels trade to Lancaster, Liverpool, &c.

3 G 3

CARRIERS BY LAND.
To Kendal, Edw. Carr, Mon. dep. 8 mng.; arr. 9 evg.——Joseph Clark, Edw. Harrison, Mary Lupton, Wed. and Sat. dep. 8 mng. arr. 8 evg.
(Stephen Carr & Walter Berry, on the arrival of vessels at Arnside Quay, carry goods to their destination)
To Hest Bank, Tobias Hutchinson.
To Lancaster, Saml. Atkinson, dep. 3 mng. arr. 9 evg.
To Manchester, (from the King's Arms) John Smith, dep. Sat. 7 evg.
To Ulverston & Cartmel, John Pickstall, from the Royal Oak, Sat.

CROSTHWAITE AND LYTH.
Marked 1 reside at *Bowland Bridge;* 2, *Church Quarter;* 3, *Church Town;* 4, *Crosthwaite Green;* 5, *How;* 6, *Hubbersty Head;* 7, *in Lyth Quarter;* 8, *Pool Bank;* 9, *Raw;* 10, *Tarn Side;* 11, *Town End Quarter.*
9 Alderson Alex. shoemaker
8 Barrow John, wood hoop manufacturer
4 Bell John, shoemaker
10 Benson Mrs. Agnes
4 Benson Thomas, grocer
2 Clark John, castrator, Town yeat
4 Clemeson Thomas, wheelwright and joiner
2 Dixon Rev. John, assistant curate and master of the free school, Cartmel fold
4 Dixon Joshua, wheelwright
2 Eglin George, paper mfr. Hill top
2 Eglin & Roberts and Co. paper mfrs.
3 Garnett Mrs. Margaret
1 Harrison Jas. blacksmith
1 Hodgson Jas. vict. Hare and Hounds
Lucas George, wheelwright, Haycotc

MILNTHORP DIRECTORY.

POST-MASTER, John Postlethwaite.—Letters from the North and South arrive from Burton in Kendal at 30 min. past 2 mg. and are despatched at 10 min. before 7 evg.— *Ulverstone Mail,* arr. 30 min. past 6 evg. and dep. 3 mg.

Adlington Miss Sarah, New row
Armstrong Thomas, horse breaker, New row
Baines John, hatter
Banks Mr. Wm. New row
Barrow James, gentleman, New row
Barton Mrs. Margaret
Baxter Richard, nail mfr.
Blewert Mrs. Eleanor, Harmony hill
Clark Thomas, farmer
Clarke Mrs. Rachael
Cragg Mrs. Elizabeth
Dixon Mr. John
Fearon Jph. tanner & tawer
Gawthrop Mr. Thomas
Green Mrs. Margaret
Hancock Mrs. Mary, New row
Harrop Miss, New row
Hird Mrs. Alice, New row
Hodgson Mrs. Mary
Holmes John, sen. land agent
Holme John, jun. farmer
Hoyle Rev. Giles, Independent minister
Huddleston Mrs. Mary
Lamenby Wm. excise officer
Myers Mrs. Elizabeth
North Mr. Edward, New row
Pitt Wm. bookkeeper
Postlethwaite John, wine & spirit merchant
Redhead John, bookkeeper

Rowes John, governor of the incorporated workhouse
Salisbury Mrs. Elizabeth, Belvedere cottage
Salisbury Thomas, solicitor, Belvedere cottage
Sanderson Edward, clog and patten maker, New row
Sawrey Mr. Edward, New row
Squires Mrs. Ann
Taylor George, brazier and tinplate worker
Towers Isaac, gentleman
Turner Mr. James
Turner Wm. paper mfr.
Wainhouse Mr. Edward
Watson Miss Eliz. New row
Widdup Mrs. Ellen
ACADEMIES.
Bentham Godfrey, (national)
Clark Betsy
Hayton Mrs. (ladies' bdg.)
Myers Miss Eleanor, (ladies' day)
Woodburn John
AUCTIONEERS.
Armistead Henry
Bainbridge Thomas
Reed John, Harforth
BLACK AND WHITE-SMITHS.
Gibson Robert
Hird William
BOOT AND SHOE MAKERS.
Cragg Isaac

Hadwen William
Saul Richard
Towers Richard
BUTCHERS.
Briggs Thomas, and Burton in Kendal
Eggleston John
Wilson Edward, and Kendal
GROCERS AND TEA DEALERS.
Atkinson Sampson
Boyd John
Bullman Thomas
Johnson John
Mason George
Nelson Richard
Whitaker George, (and iron-monger and seedsman)
Winder Emanuel Shepherd, (& cast iron warehouse)
HOTELS, INNS, AND PUBLIC HOUSES.
Bull's Head, Wm. Whormby
Cross Key's Inn, Elizabeth Hudson
King's Arms, Thomas Bainbridge
Royal Oak, Isaac Clemmett
White Lion, Wm. Thompson
JOINERS, CABINET MAKERS & WHEELWRIGHTS.
Marked 1, *are Joiners and Cabinet Makers; and* 2, *are Joiners & Wheelwrights.*
1 Cornthwaite George

11

PUBLIC ESTABLISHMENTS.

Kitching Memorial Institute, J. G. D. Whitaker, sec.; L. G. Powell, treas.; William Thompson, caretaker
Police Station
Milnthorpe Mental Home, J. J. Kerr, master; Mrs. Kerr, matron; J. R. Caldwell M.B., Ch.B. St. Andrews, medical officer

PUBLIC OFFICERS.

Certifying Factory Surgeon, John R. Caldwell M.B., Ch.B. St. Andrews, Stoneleigh
Medical Officer & Public Vaccinator Milnthorpe District, South Westmorland Guardians Committee, John R. Caldwell M.B., Ch.B. St. Andrews, Stoneleigh

(For T N's see general list of Private Residents at end of book.)
Atkins James, Yew bank
Caldwell John R., M.B. Stoneleigh
Cameron James Kenneth M.B. Overdale
Constable Alfred W. Rock Heath
Dean Rev. Frederick M.A.Camb., LL.B.Dub. Morningside
Dobson Percy, Lane Edge
Downing Mrs. Ivy house
Elburn Mrs. Fleet house
Elleray Richard H. Miln hall
Gamble Rev. John Leonard M.A. (vicar), Vicarage
Harrison-Broadley J. H., Parkside
Hildred George, Hay close, Ackenthwaite
Hodgson Harry O. Ryley field
Hodgson Richard O. Harmony hill
Jackson Thomas, Ormandy, Ackenthwaite house
Kilpatrick Mrs. Heatherlyn
Langhorn Robert, Park road
McIntire Walter T., F.S.A.Scot. St. Anthony's
McLeod Mrs. E. M., J.P. Flowerden
Mashiter Edward, The Square
Mashiter John, Maymyo
Miles Arthur John, Laburnam house
Newsham George, Glasgow house
Scott Miss, Oakfield
Scott William, Kirkgate
Sharp Miss, Myengarth
Shaw William, Ackenthwaite
Thompson Henry, The Square
Walker Thomas, Greystone
Whitley Robert, Lyndene
Wilson Mason, Milncrest
Wilson William, Park road
Woods Hanley Raby, Park road

COMMERCIAL.

Early closing day, Thursday.
Marked thus ° farm 150 acres or over.
Airey Thos. basket mkr
Barr Saml. statnr. & post office
Bateman Jas. registrar of births, deaths & marriages Milnthorpe sub-district, Kendal Registration district & relieving & vaccination officer Southern district, South Westmorland Guardians Committee & school attendance officer
Brown Geo E. tobccnst
Brown Wm. Geo. shopkpr
Burch Frank, butcher. T N 69
Burton, Milnthorpe & Carnforth Agricultural Society (T. B. Jackson, sec)
Caldwell Jn. R., M.B., Ch.B.St. Andrews, surgn. & certifying factory surgn. medical officer & public vaccinator Milnthorpe district, South Westmorland Guardians Committee & medical officer Milnthorpe Mental Homes

Cameron Jas. Kenneth M.B., Ch.B. L'pool (firm,Caldwell & Cameron), physcn. & surgn. Overdale. T N 54
Clark Bros. butchers. T N 40
Clarke Edwd. carrier
Constable Alfd. Whittam, cycle agent
Cooper Geo. assistant engnr. & surveyor to South Westmorland Rural District Council. T N 42
Cottam & Hodgson, agricultural seed mers.; T A "Cottam, Milnthorpe;" T N 22
Coward Isaac, boot & shoe dlr
Daish's Ltd. grocers. T N 5
District Bank Ltd.(The) (sub-branch) (Wm. Wilcock, mngr.) (open mon. tues. wed. & fri. 10 a.m. to 3 p.m.; thurs. 10 a.m. to 12 noon); head office, Spring gdns. Manchester
Dobson John (Milnthorpe) Ltd. comb mkrs. Bela mill. T A "Combs;" T N 55; A B C Code, 5th Edition, Bentley's & private
Dobson Harry Cragg, ironmngr
Douthwaite Joseph & Sons, motor engineers, Bridge end. T N 16
Douthwaite Wm. O. blacksmith, Ackenthwaite
Eason Rd. grocer
Fawcett Jn. & Sons, motor engnrs. The Square & Beetham rd. T A "Fawcetts;" T N 6
Fleming Chas. Norman, confctnr
Fleming Geo. saddler
Garnett Jas.Wm. frmr.Ackenthwaite
Hayes Albert Isaac, boot maker
Hayes Robert, coal agent
Heath Geo. fried fish dlr
Henderson Jas. motor engnr. T N 65
Higginbottom Matthew, paper agt. T N 36
Hodgson Nelson & Scott Limited, builders. T N 28
Hodgson Harry C. seed merchant, see Cottam & Hodgson
Hodgson Richard Ormrod, haulage contractor. T N 53
Holliday Richard, farmer, Crag yeat
Holmes Frank, painter
Hyde Wm. Harold, carrier
Jackson T. O. & J. K. solicitors & commissioners for oaths. T N 86
James Margt. & Ann(Misses),shopkprs
Kay Oliver & Co. merchants
Kendal Co-operative Society Limited (branch). T N 71
Kitching Memorial Institute (J. G. D. Whitaker, sec.; L. G. Powell, treas.; Wm. Thompson, caretaker)
Martins Bank Ltd. (sub-branch) (Arth. W. Sutcliffe, mngr.) (open daily except sat.) (T N 8); head office, 4 Water st. Liverpool 2

Relieving & Vaccination Officer, Southern District,South Westmorland Guardians Committee & Registrar of Births, Deaths & Marriages, Milnthorpe Sub-District, Kendal Registration District, James Bateman

CARRIERS TO:—

Kendal—William Harold Hyde, daily; Edward Clarke, tues., fri. & sat.; Richard Emanuel Sumpton, wed. & sat
Lancaster—Richard Emanuel Sumpton, fri
Ulverston & Grange—Richard Emanuel Sumpton, wed

Railway Station (L. M. & S)
Conveyance.—Motor omnibuses run daily to Kendal & Lancaster from The Square

Mashiter John, clerk to Milnthorpe Sub-Committee Westmorland Local Pensions Committee, Park road
Mashiter Walt. Edwd. tailor. T N 70
Mental Home (The) (J. J. Kerr, master; Mrs. Kerr, matron; for medical staff see Official section)
Midland Bank Ltd. (sub-branch) (Wm. Kilvert Howard, mngr.) (open mon. tues. wed. & fri. 10 a.m. to 3 p.m.; thurs. 10 a.m. to 12 noon); head office, Poultry, London E C 2
Milnthorpe Gas, Coal, Coke & Lime Co. Ltd. (Robert Hayes, sec)
Milnthorpe Rooms Co. Ltd. (Geo. Leslie Wilson, eec)
Ministry of Labour Employment Exchange (Geo. Hildred, mngr)
Moss Geo. newsagt
Naylor R. O., A.S.A.A. incorporated accntnt. (attends wed)
Newsham Ernest, draper, Church st
Newsham Geo. maltster. T N 24
Newsham Jacob, coal dlr
Powell Leslie G. solicitor & commissioner for oaths (firm, Talbot, Rheam & Webster), clerk to the justices, steward of the manor of Burton & agent for Heversham Vicarage lands. T N 63
Reed Alfd. Hind, Station inn. T N 84
Revell Herbt. E. Cross Keys hotel. T N 15
Scott Samuel, farmer, Crag yeat, Ackenthwaite
Semple Arth. plumber
Sharp Jn. Rowland,boot mkr. TN 37
Sheldon Walt. H., M.P.S. chemist
Slack Lily (Miss), district nurse, The Square
Smith Eric David, dentist (attends mon. 2 to 7 p.m)
Stainton Thos. motor engnr. Church st. T N 34
Story Norman, Bull's Head hotel. T N 33
Sumpton Rd. Emanuel, beer retlr. & carrier. T N 60
Talbot, Rheam & Webster (L. G. Powell), solctrs. T N 63
Thompson Jessie (Mrs.), draper, Church st
Thompson Jn. Wm. plumber
Walker Agnes (Mrs.), café
Whitaker J. G. D. solicitor. T N 103
Whitehead Thomas Geo. fishmonger
Whiteley Harold, hairdrser
°Whitfield Thos. farmer, Bridge End farm
Wilson William Geo. & Son, joiners
Wilson John, farmer, Crosby lodge, Ackenthwaite
Wilson Mary E. (Mrs.), confctnr
Woods Hanley, confectioner

Extract from
Kelly's Directory 1934.

Front cover of Church Magazine
from which the adverts opposite (p13) came.

The
PARISH MAGAZIN
Monthly Notes of Church Activities in Beetham, Crosscrake, Heversham, Holme, Levens and Milnthorp

NOVEMBER, 1950.   PRICE

MILNTHORPE CHURCH

BEETHAM	- Rev. C. Williams	'Phone Milnthorpe 1
CROSSCRAKE	- Rev. J. A. M. Johnstone	Sedgwick 3
HEVERSHAM	- Rev. W. A. Cleghorn	Milnthorpe 1
HOLME	- Rev. H. Burnyeat	
LEVENS	- Rev. G. W. Ellison	Sedgwick 2
MILNTHORPE	- Rev. C. H. Lee	Milnthorpe 24

In every case the address is "The Vicarage."

Advertisements from Milnthorpe's
Parish Magazine 1949 .
'Uncle Alf' Read's Pork Pie 'factory'
was in buildings at Milnthorpe Station.

SUPPORT your Local Tradespeople and your Local Passenger Transport Operators—

"BOOK THAT OUTING WITH"

DALLAM

Proprietors—Messrs JOHN FAWCETT & SONS
The Square — Tel. 6 — Milnthorpe

On account of my Health I have now turned my Window Cleaning over to my son, T. Walker, and hope that all my customers will give him the same good will and patronage I have always had. Any enquiries sent to this address will receive his personal attention.
CHURCH STREET, MILNTHORPE

CROSS KEYS HOTEL MILNTHORPE

RESIDENTIAL · LUNCHEONS · TEAS · ETC.
PROPRIETRESS—M. V. CAIRNS   TELEPHONE : MILNTHORPE 15

E & B
PROMPT
RADIO
REPAIRS
Main Street, Milnthorpe

W. Nicholson
PLUMBER
Sanitary and Heating Engineer
" SUNNY GHYLL "
Heversham Road, Milnthorpe
Estimates Free   'Phone 160

J. L. ION
MOTOR & ENGINEERING
REPAIRS. Modern Equipment
Church Street, Milnthorpe
Telephone : 34

AUDREY'S
THE SHOP
Milnthorpe Folk
. . *GO TO*
ALL WELCOME
'Phone : Milnthorpe 108

The **HEVERSHAM HOTEL . . .**
UNDER NEW MANAGEMENT
THIS Hotel has now been entirely refurnished & decorated and is open for Morning coffee, luncheons,
Afternoon Teas & dinners.
Suppers 10 p.m.—Midnight
Tables bookable by 'phone
MILNTHORPE 59
BROCHURE AND TARIFF ON APPLICATION
PRINCE'S WAY · MILNTHORPE

Shop at . .
DAISH'S
and get . .
Value for Money

FUEL (all types) **SAWN LOGS**
(Registered customers)
Westmorland Waterworn Limestone Rockery
Sea Washed Turf for Bowling Greens and Tennis Courts, etc.
SANDSIDE COAL Co. Ltd.
SANDSIDE, WESTMORLAND
Telephone Milnthorpe 25 & 26

Visit the . .
CINEMA
MILNTHORPE
Mon., Tues., Fri., & Sat.
Seats Booked at G. Brown's Tel. 20

A. Semple & Son
DECORATORS & PLUMBERS
MILNTHORPE

AUDREY'S
THE SHOP
Milnthorpe Folk
. . *GO TO*
ALL WELCOME
'Phone : Milnthorpe 108

TOBACCO & CIGARETTES · SWEETS
CHOCOLATES · MINERALS
—THE—
"BON-BON"
—Mrs. J. H. Woods—
DAILY NEWSPAPERS · PERIODICALS
STATIONERY
MILNTHORPE

It's a pleasure to be "hungry" when
you've **Uncle Alf's Pies**
"DAINTY AS EVER"

COMPLETE OUTFITS FOR HEVERSHAM GRAMMER SCHOOL
BREECHES A SPECIALITY
FOR EVERYTHING IN MENS & BOYS WEAR
Mashiter & Son. [J. W. Cordukes]
TAILORS AND GENTS OUTFITTERS
TEL. 70   **MILNTHORPE**   TEL. 70

Milnthorpe is an 'in-between place' in seeming to be not quite a town nor yet a village. Its population in 1996 was estimated as 2050 bigger than the 'town' of Kirkby Lonsdale -1925-but smaller than the 'village' of Arnside -2250.

Historically Milnthorpe was one of the bigger towns in Westmorland with a population of 1600 in 1841. The figure had fallen to below 1000 by 1921 when the place became known as a 'village'.

Socially Milnthorpe has the 'feel' of a village as, perhaps, is indicated by this photograph of May Day revels taken in 1916 just at the time when many local lads were being slaughtered in the First World War. But in bad times as in good there has always been some scope for amusement.

Hence any illustration of Milnthorpe's history must depict fun and games.

2: Milnthorpe's Story - above all - is about People

Fortunately since the invention of photography Milnthorians have not minded being snapped for posterity - individually or in groups, formally or informally, at work or at play, wearing their Sunday best or workaday wear. Some of the folk depicted are known, some are not - but all illustrate something of the way of life in a Westmorland village in former times.

Village lads in Dallam Park about 1910 - note polished boots and stiff Eton Collars.

Mashiter's window sill serving as a seat for the Semple family about 1900. No one has been able to explain why they needed a lantern on what was obviously a sunny day.

The Mashiter family posing in the garden of Fern Cottage, Park Road in 1905.

Left to Right Mrs John Mashiter with her daughter Addie on her knee. Mrs Roger Mashiter, Ernest Mashiter, John Mashiter and Roger Mashiter.

Ernest was a clever lad who went on to Oxford from Heversham Grammar School. By donning a mortar board at the age of ten he obviously seems to have anticipated his later academic prowess.

Milnthorpians are country folk. Here we see Johnny Wilson at Milnthorpe Station with his milk float from Crosby Lodge Farm in c.1934. His passengers are Christopher and Elizabeth Audland. In 1986 'Sir Christopher' became Milnthorpe's first post medieval knight, an accolade he earned in the Diplomatic Service.

Wedding Group at Milton Moor Farm in 1908.

Seated - the bride Miss Sarah Inman and her groom Mr Sydney Corrie.

Behind - Mr Tom Inman - the bride's father, Miss Edith Inman - the bride's sister and bridesmaid. The best man is now unknown.

Tom Nicholson - postman in 1920 photographed outside Parkside. Tom also lit the village gas lamps trailing on winter nights up and down Milnthorpe's lanes and streets holding a lighted taper and, over his shoulder, a short ladder which he used to check the mantles in the lanterns. (left)

Miss Wilson with Jack Black and terrier outside the Black's cottage on Haverflatts Lane. Most of the Haverflatts Lane cottages and Spring Cottage have now been demolished. (right)

Young Milnthorpians. Mrs Atkinson and baby Wilf outside Spring Cottage, Park Road 1906.

Abraham Douthwaite with his cow outside The Smithy, Ackenthwaite in c.1900. Abraham was 'renowned for his deep opinions and uncertain temper'. Modern experts believe he had a poor choice of cattle, judging by the beast in the photograph.

3: The Port and Milnthorpe Sands

Milnthorpe Sands from Haverbrack in c.1890 showing the river Bela meandering into the Kent estuary and, also, the Bela Viaduct on the Furness Railway's Arnside to Hincaster branch line. Summer House points juts out beyond the viaduct.

Milnthorpe lies mainly in a valley so that drumlins to the west of the village conceal the fact that the final tidal reaches of Morecambe Bay are less than half a mile from its centre.

In Mashiter's Post Card of Milnthorpe from the Firs of about 1890 the Bay can just be glimpsed in the top left hand corner.

The port's activities were concentrated at 'The Milnthorpe Sandside'. This area is called the Dixies a name probably deriving from the Viking word 'dika' for a channel. In Allom and Rose's engraving of 'Milnthorpe Sands Westmoreland' of c.1826 vehicles are seen splashing through the channels at low tide while a cart laden with peats dug from beds at Foulshaw on the far side of the estuary is coming up the wharf. One of the fishermen in the foreground is carrying a shrimp net. The thatched roofed cottage was the home of the Sandside Ferryman while the taller house known as Crown Cottage (dated AIT 1728) was a Custom's House.

Allom's engraving Milnthorpe sands at the Dixies (Sandside) c.1820

The Summer House on Summerhouse Point at the mouth of the Bela was built about 1780 on the site of tollhouse from where dues were levied by the Wilson's of Dallam Tower at the rate of 'every boat that comes up the river pays four pence for unloading'. (left)

The Summer House was used by the public as a changing room for bathing until it was demolished by the Wilson's in 1898 during an acrimonious dispute with Milnthorpe Parish Council about access rights to the shore and to Haverbrack common. Its stones were used to build the **washhouse** at the Dallam Tower North Lodge seen on the extreme right of this picture. (below)

21

The White Barn on Harmony Hill   photographed by Berry in c.1970 when it was used as a Council depot . Although nearly a mile from the Port's main activities at Sandside the barn was originally the Port's bonded warehouse. It is now used by TT Carpets. The chestnut tree behind was planted about 1815 when a common called Milnthorpe Green was enclosed. It blew down in 1982 shortly before the road was widened but descendants grown from its conkers were planted on the land and have given their name to a new housing development called Chestnut Park.

'Spike Driving' on the Bela about 1900. The bearded man wearing the top hat is believed to be Walter Berry of Birkett's Farm . He had been one of the Port's main carriers until shipping was prevented from coming close to Milnthorpe after 1857 when the construction of the Arnside railway viaduct caused the navigable channels to silt up.

THE SANDSIDE FERRY BOAT, WHICH WAS SWAMPED BY THE TIDE, SEPT 2ND, 1905. AND SIX OUT OF THE ELEVEN PASSENGERS DROWNED.

The ferry service moved from the Dixies to the Ship Inn and continued until the disaster of 1905 referred to in the caption. Several bodies were not found immediately and the search went on until nightfall. While the searchers were reviving themselves at The Ship a spectator rushed in to say that a head could be seen floating in the ebbing tide. Whereupon a boat was commandeered and rowed drunkenly into the middle of the bay where a turnip was 'rescued'.

Westmorland's Little Blackpool.

Milnthorpe Sands at St. John's Cross in 1934. One of the reasons why Milnthorpe got a church was that 'multitudes of people from the country around resort to the sands during ye bathing season' and the vicar thought that the opportunity to hear a sermon would be a suitable extra diversion. Scenes like these, (above and left) were photographed during every heat wave until the 1960's when foreign holidays and urban leisure centres took their toll on the British seaside.

4: Dallam Tower

Dallam Tower is the manor house for Milnthorpe although it is situated in Beetham parish. Allom and Rose's engraving of Haymaking in Dallam Park dates from just after the house was enlarged by the Kendal architect George Webster for George Smyth Wilson in 1826. They added the cupolas on the side wings, which sometimes have caused the house to be called inaccurately 'Dallam Towers'. The name tower derives from a medieval Pele tower, which occupied an adjacent site.

Dallam Tower as built for Daniel Wilson MP between 1720-22.

The front door was always on the first floor but since the Webster alterations the lower floor has been disguised by a terrace, which completely hides the full size downstairs sash windows.

The New Bridge, Milnthorpe.

Dallam Tower 'New' Bridge with the Bela railway viaduct beyond in c.1900.

The 'New Bridge', also designed by Webster in c.1820, was built when the Sandside to Milnthorpe main road was diverted from running through Dallam Park to the north side of the Bela. The high arch was to allow shipping to reach landing staithes on the river bank.

The return from the Westmorland Assizes of High Sheriff Edward George Wilson (sixth from the right) to Dallam Tower in 1886 accompanied by chaplain, javelin men, trumpeters and footmen all dressed in the Wilson livery.

Edward was a bachelor and on his death the estate was inherited by his sisters. When they died within a few weeks of each other in 1891 Dallam devolved to a somewhat distant cousin Maurice Bromley who added Wilson to his name. Eventually he inherited his father's baronetcy becoming known to everyone in Milnthorpe as 'Serm Oriss'. Since 1891 Milnthorpe has had only two squires Maurice and his nephew Brigadier C.E. (Teddy) Tryon-Wilson who inherited in 1956. The title does not go with Dallam and is now borne by Sir Henry Bromley who lives in South Africa.

Horse teams 'Leading timber' through the Bela. Dallam Park c.1914.

Sir Maurice Bromley-Wilson with his beagles in the top park about 1913.

The Dallam Otter Hound hunting their prey in the Park.

Dallam was famous (or notorious) for its pack of otter hounds. This shot of the kennels is believed to date from the 1880's.

Until the 1960's when the pack was disbanded following the abolition of otter hunting the hounds' baying during the mid day 'feeding of the dogs' could be heard all over Milnthorpe.

5: Park Road

Milnthorpe's western road leading to Dallam Park is called Park Road. In this 1920 photograph John Dobson is clearing a drain prior to the laying of tarmac. Motor traffic was now common but note the evidence of horses!

Spring Cottage, Park Road c.1910 (above).
The spring is on the right . Park View (on the left with the bay window) was built in 1871 on the site of Milnthorpe's last thatched cottages. The Bela Forge houses now occupy the south side (right) of this scene.

A rare photograph of Semples the decorators Paint and Ironmongers shop. The building to the side was once the Port of Milnthorpe's Customs house.

Park Road c.1910. The trees were cut down in c.1945. The eighteenth century Dallam Tower cottages (left) were occupied by estate workers. As late the 1950's an older occupant was seen to bob a curtsey as Sir Maurice Bromley-Wilson went by!

Higher up Park Road also about 1910. The Co-operative Stores are on the right .

Milnthorpe's 'Industrial Co-operative Society was founded in 1862 and later amalgamated with the Kendal society. Milnthorpe Co-op closed in 1984 since when almost every body from Milnthorpe has continued to use the premises -once- as they were taken over by Fishwick's Funeral Services.

Close up of the Co-op. William Milwood the manager stands proudly on the doorstep below the soap advert soon after the shop was opened in 1906. Previously the stores had been based lower down Park Road and before then on the corner of Church Street and Main Street.

Douthwaite's Bridge End Garage in 1928. Originally a smithy and before then the site of an iron forge the garage had only recently expanded into the former barn and shippon.
L to R. Tommy Burrows, Jo Douthwaite, Bill Douthwaite.

The car in the doorway was known as the 'old hundred weight' because its number 5656 added up to 112 as in 112 pounds one cwt.

A lost corner of Park Road opposite the Co-op in c.1910. On the right Langhorne's house; on the left work buildings at various times used by Hinds and Hayes Shoemakers and by Walter Mashiter the tailor. The fine water worn limestone gateposts were removed in 1983 but some cobbles still survive here.

View of Park Road from Main Street c.1890 showing the old low built Post Office. The window cleaners (or painters) are maintaining the King's Arms.

View of Park Road c.1910 showing the new post office built in 1897, the Cross Keys on the left and in the left corner a horse standing in front of the 'painters' (penthouse) outside the Royal Oak. Flowerden House on the right was rebuilt by the Bindloss family in 1881; the buildings to its west were demolished in 1924 to create the modern cross roads.

6: Main Street

Main Street from a post card sent on 18th February 1908 by Jim Sisson to his sweetheart Maria Ingram of Sedgwick who received it on the same day!

On the south side of the street can be seen the full façade of the Royal Oak with the bar entrance on the left and the 'painters' shelter on the right. On the north side a stretch of typical Milnthorpe cobbles fronts the District Bank and Flemming's Café - all of which were swept away in 1924 - so that Flowerden's sash window facing down the street, now looks onto the traffic lights at the Cross Roads. The 'Fagin-like' figure is 'Toffee Johnny Gray' who might have been a murderer! (see War Section) while the toddler with the hobby horse is possibly Dorothy Flemming or her brother Norrie.

Main Street, Milnhorpe.

Main Street c.1910 with St Thomas School of 1866 on the right and Stoneleigh built by the Misses Saul in 1873 on the left.

In 1911 Main Street was the first Milnthorpe road to be tarmaced. By 1917 Westmorland County Council had tarmacadamed all the main highways as far as the Lancashire border at Hale. By 1930 Westmorland claimed to have more cars per head of population than any place on earth!

Map from Benjamin West's *Guide to the Lakes* fourth edition 1789 showing Main Road through Burton, pre 'A6' turnpike through Yealands to 'Milnthorp' and over the sands routes.

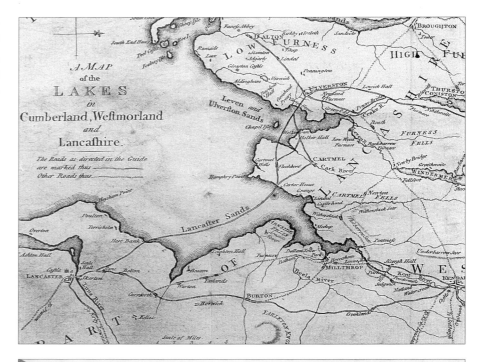

Main Street c.1910. On the left the entrance to Twine Walk (where a rope works were situated between c.1800 and 1870), then Claughton's butchers and Atkinson's shoe shop; in the centre T&H Richmond's grocers. (left)

HANNONY SQUARE, MILNTHORPE.

Harmony Hill in c.1890 and an example of the misspelling of an ancient village place name whose origins no one knows. Carr Yard top right is called after a family of port carriers who lived there in the eighteenth century. Harmony Hall on the right was built by a Milnthorpe sea captain Joseph Fayrer between 1790 and 1810. (below). The building on the left is the Dame School built by Mary Anne Mason in 1850.

39

7: The Square

The Square before 1865 showing the Lock Up built beneath the Market Cross. This correctional facility was provided by the Milnthorpe Prosecution Society following disturbances caused by an influx of navvies who were constructing the main railway line to the east of the village in the 1840's. Why the law keepers chose to go to all the trouble of pulling down the already ancient Cross and re-erecting it on top of a prison cell cannot now be fathomed. The Lock Up was demolished soon after a Police Station opened in Police Square in 1866.

Back End Cattle Fair c.1900. Cattle arriving the night before the fair were kept in nearby meadows where residents were allowed to milk them at dawn. (left)

The Square c .1905. The bearded man on the left is believed to be Happy Jack Fawcett founder of the fortunes of one of Milnthorpe's more enterprising families.

41

The Square c.1890 showing Vine House (now the Spa) on the left and white washed cottages to the extreme right on the site of two sandstone fronted houses erected by Edward Mashiter in 1906.

Outline to show places on the c.1847 photograph of Milnthorpe opposite. The photograph was probably taken from the viewing platform on the roof of Harmony Hall.

KEY TO DIAGRAM

1. Haverbrack
2. Dallam1
3. Kent Estuary
4. Cartmell Fell
5. Birkett's Farm
6. Barrel workshop.
7. Kings Arms
8. Old Flowerden house
9. Fleet House
10. Cottages on site of Stoneleigh
11. Mallow House
12. Green Cottage
13. Barn/warehouse

14. Coach and Horses
15. Bodkin Hall.
16. Vine House
17. Royal Oak.
18. The 'painters'.
19. Main Street.
20. Cross Keys
21. White Lion Inn.
22. Fish Shop (site of Institute)
23. Strands Meadow
24. Strands Cottages formerly Low mills
25. Paper Mill.

26. Bull's Head.
27. Malt Kiln
28. Cross View
29. Royal Oak Assembly Room
30. Market Cross
31. The Square
32. The Green.
33. Ash tree cut down in 1875

Milnthorpe in c.1847.

This is not only the oldest photograph of Milnthorpe but is also old by national standards. We can date it fairly accurately as it shows the Market Cross without the Lock Up (erected c. 1847) and Bodkin Hall on the site of St Thomas' School. As Bodkin Hall was demolished before the Lock Up in 1866 the photograph must date from before the Lock Up was built. Get it?

The May Fair 1908.

Although only cattle are shown in this picture other animals were sold. Horses were put through their paces outside the Cross Keys, sheep were penned on the north side of the church and geese were tethered to the railings of Laburnum House.

Proclamation of an Old English Fair to raise funds for the Church in 1934.

Bill Garnett is reading the proclamation with John Mashiter on his right and the Rev J. L. Gamble on his left.

44

Close up of the rockery stones round the Fountain c.1948 with L to R: Sheila Wheatman, Alma Black, Marion Sadler, Muriel Prickett, and Marjorie Walker. (right)

Square in 1920 from the Church Tower showing the back of the old Royal Oak. The rockery stones surround the village well known as the Fountain. They were placed there about 1890 after Miss Rawlinson fell in the well while coming from Evensong on a dark night. The Fountain was concreted over in 1940 after a circus elephant fell while drinking here. As no elephant subsequently has come to any harm the Parish Council in 2000 has dared to open up the Fountain again. But the name of The Jumbo Chinese Take Away is a reminder of the accident (below).

Milnthorpe

Square in 1930 showing the new Bull's Head garages and George Flemming's saddlers shop on the former Royal Oak site.

Milnthorpe.

North East Corner of the Square

c.1930 showing the common lodging house known as the 'Padding Can' after one Paddy O'Connor its keeper in the 1890's. The buildings, pump (to the left) and the trees were cleared away in 1946 to provide an entrance to the Firs Road Council Estate.

8: The Crossroads and Church Street

This photograph of the triumphal arch   erected to greet Edward George Wilson on his return from the Appleby Assizes in 1886 also shows the east side of Church Street before the cross roads were made. On the right is the King's Arms and directly ahead is the Cross Keys named after the badge of St Peter the patron saint of Heversham Church to which the street led.

As the largest hostelry between Kendal and Lancaster the 'Keys' was still important but its greatest days were over. During the coaching era its landlady Mrs Hudson received the King of Saxony, the Russian Tsarevich (later Alexander II) and Queen Adelaide widow of King William IV plus innumerable Lords and ladies.

The Royal Oak seen from Park Road in c. 1920. On the right just down from the Cross Keys is the Bon Bon sweet shop and newsagents belonging to Handley Woods. Next door was formerly a tavern known as The Wagon and Horses where humbler travellers partook refreshment while the carriage trade patronised the Cross Keys. (below)

Church Street during the Coronation Celebrations of Edward VII in 1902. The Coronation had been planned for June but was postponed at the last moment when King went down with an append-icitis. But as the 'ham had been boiled and might have gone off and every-thing was ready' Miln-thorpe children still got their Coronation tea which was repeated in August when the King was crowned and when the village's own proc-essions took place

The Blue Row in Church Street

c.1920. The row was built between 1820 and 1830 by the Whig/Liberal Building Society to provide a 40 shilling free hold, which gave voting rights. Blue was the colour of the Westmorland liberals and yellow the local Tory colour until 1983.

At the house on the extreme left James Wilson was murdered in 1824. His battered body had a burnt hand and foot and bruises and blood on the head above the temples. Although warrants were issued by the Home Secretary Robert Peel there were, apparently, no suspects and the culprit was never found.

Milnthorpe Hill 'top o' Church Street ' c.1940. Note lack of traffic, gas lamps, erected 1866, and the telegraph poles first installed in 1851. The gas lamps were replaced by electric lamps in 1949 and most of the poles were removed in the 1960's.

"Top of the Hill' on Church Street in 1922. Although there is but one charabanc in view the recent increase in motor traffic had caused the authorities to turn down an application from John Mashiter for a front drive to his new house 'Maymyo' - seen nearing completion on the right. Only in 1998 after the A6 road had been 'de-trunked' was a direct access from the main road permitted for a new dwelling built on the 'Maymyo' tennis court.

Incidentally the tennis court was built on extra land which John Mashiter had been forced to buy, after George Wilson 'with whom he had never been the best of friends' had threatened to build inferior houses in front of the Mashiter mansion. Allegedly he had to pay £600 - about £50,000 in the values of 80 years later! But the tennis court was got on the cheap: it was dug out of the banking and levelled by unemployed labourers working only for their dinner - which was 'stew every day'!

9: Beetham Road

Beetham Road c.1914 showing the Police Station built in 1910, the 10MPH signs and the buildings which obstructed the through route from Beetham Road to Church Street. The old Bull's Head is on the right on a site now used as the present Bull's Head's car park.

Walkers Bela Café was converted out of the cricket pavilion when the village team transferred to the playing field in the 1920's. Nevertheless The Ashes and The Willows housing development recently built in the area allude to its former use.

The Crossroads from Beetham Road about 1930 showing the Kitching Memorial Reading Rooms (of 1881) known an The Institute on the left and Mr Flemming's Café and the new Bull's Head recently rebuilt for A. J. Miles of Whitwell Marks Brewery on the right. The old Bull's Head was on the car park bottom right and part of its wall was left as a buttress to hold up the Public Rooms. Prior to the old pub's demolition this part of Beetham Road was said to be the narrowest point on the route from London to Glasgow. Note the weighing machine outside Mrs Gould's shop. The District Bank occupied the Institute shop on the extreme left. The Virginia creeper clad Flowerden House built for the Bindloss family in 1880 was currently the home of Dr. and Mrs Macleod née Argles. Sergeant Aikrigg is patiently waiting to direct non-existent traffic.

Close up of Ben Aikrigg standing on his little dais. Traces of the demolished east side of Church Street can be seen on the wall of Flowerden.

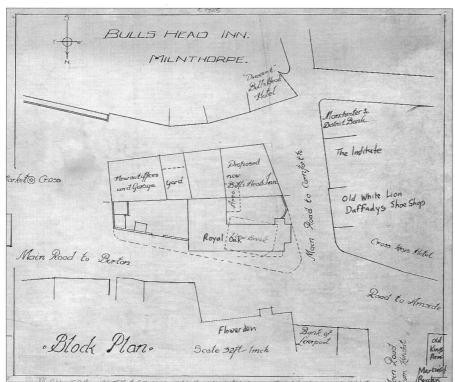

Architects plan for the rebuilding of the Bull's Head showing the alignment of roads and buildings prior to the creation of the Crossroads in c.1924.

Milnthorpe's first Church.
Because Milnthorpe was served by the old Parish Church at Heversham the first place of worship was a Non-conformist Chapel of the Independents, which opened in the building on the left on the 18th March 1820. Later it was taken over by the Methodists who used it until their purpose built chapel was established on Beetham Road in 1904. After it ceased to be a chapel the building became a house called The Pillars although to the delight of bright school children in the 1950's a name plate in Woolworth's' plastic lettering called the dwelling 'The Pillers'.

Harvest thanksgiving decorations in the old chapel.

The foundation stones laying service for 'The new Wesleyan Church' 1904.

One of the younger members of the congregation was Doris Mashiter who in 1998 became the first lifelong resident of Milnthorpe to become 100. Everybody hopes - and expects - Doris to be present at the Chapel's centenary!

The new 'Chapel'.

A FAREWELL ADDRESS

TO THE INHABITANTS OF THE DISTRICT OF ST. THOMAS', MILNTHORPE; WHO HAVE ATTENDED THE CHURCH DURING THE FIRST TWENTY-THREE YEARS, SINCE IT WAS OPENED ON SUNDAY THE 30th JULY, 1837. OCCASIONED BY THE RESIGNATION, FROM ILLNESS OF THE LATE INCUMBENT.

Heading to the farewell address of the Rev Nicholas Padwick 28 July 1860. He was the first vicar, who built up the congregation, ended labourers Hiring Fairs on Sunday and bought Belvedere (the house to the right of the Church) to be a vicarage. His presence as a ghost is said to live on at Belvedere, which reverted to being a private house when the Heversham and Milnthorpe Anglican churches became served only by the vicar of Heversham in 1992.

(opposite - above right)
South side of the Church c.1910 showing the field which is now covered by Firs Road. St. Thomas' derives its name not from the doubting saint but from Mrs Thomasin Richardson who gave £1,000 as an endowment. The chairman of the building fund was the Rev Carus Wilson of Casterton who was vilified as Mr Brocklehurst by Charlotte Bronte in 'Jane Eyre'.

(opposite - below right)
New Bells for the Church. 1912. The old bells were given to Levens Church where they were hung in a frame in the yard and struck by hammers to summon worshippers.

North side of the Church from Main Street in 1900. The road side trees were planted to commemorate Queen Victoria's Jubilee in 1887.

Chapel Tea c.1914. The gentlemen led by Mr. Newsham fourth from the left served the ladies.

The Church's gas lit interior c.1930.

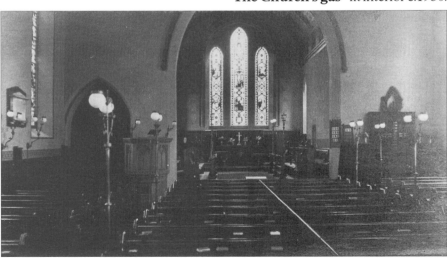

The Church Choir in 1937 when it was first robed.

Back Row L to R Rhoda Jonson, Betty Douthwaite, Lillian Taylor, Muriel Atkinson, Marion Saddler, Mrs Saddler.

Middle Row Bill Garnett (warden/verger), Eva Scott, John Pickthall, Geoff Morton, Geoff Scott, George Flemming, William Douthwaite, John Herdson, Frank White, Herbert Eccles, Annie Morton, Harold Fawcett (warden).

Front Row Jessie Thompson, Dorothy Warne, Margaret Douthwaite, Jeanette Douthwaite, John Mashiter (lay reader), Rev John L.Gamble (vicar), L.G.Powell (organist), Rotha Thompson, Elsie Eccles, Edith Wilson and Addie Pickthall.

Detail of the east end as decorated for the 150th Anniversary celebrations in 1987.

The window was given in 1872 by the Whittaker family who had made a fortune importing South American guano into the Port of Milnthorpe. It was designed by Frederick Burrow of Sandside. Pevsner in his Buildings of England called it 'bad'!

Church Choir 1949.

Top Row L to R.   Tony Thompson (verger), Peter Ellis, Peter Kirby, ? Woodhead, William Hird, Brian Broomfield, Ian Robinson, Donald Benson.

Third Row   Joyce Starkie, Pauline Thompson, Alma Black, Margery Walker, Marian Saddler, Myra Davenport, Brenda Walsh, Roda Johnson, Barbara Wilson.

Second Row   Neil Scott, Trevor Semple, Colin Gott, Geoff Scott, William Douthwaite, Leslie Wilson, Graham Woodhead, Colin Robinson,? Woodhead.

Front Row   Michael Kirby, Sheila Tauber, Mrs Hayes (organist), Rev Cyril Lee (vicar), Betty Douthwaite, Ethel Flemming, Mrs Saddler, and Frank Fothergill.

11: Homes

The earliest village homes evolved from longhouses of Anglo-Saxon times. Low Croft at Ackenthwaite is a later example.

Larger longhouses had a section for the animals and one for the humans all under the same roof but separated by a through passage. At Vine Cottage on Harmony Green the large wooden door represents the entry to a through passage while the barn next to it indicates a former agricultural use.

DALLAM PARK.

Park Side extreme right seen from Dallam Park in a post card posted on New Year's Eve 1906. Park Side dates back at least to the sixteenth century when it would have been the dwelling of a small land owner known as a 'statesman'. Since c.1800 it has belonged to the Dallam Estate serving intermittently as the Dower House or as the home of the agent

Close up of Park Side showing a range of round 'Westmorland' chimneys of c.1600.

The Cottage, Ackenthwait e currently the home of the Ladell family and shown here with the Gott family in c.1900 is typical of the next stage up from the long house. As it does not appear on Blount's map The Cottage probably dates from after 1826.

Bela Cottages, Mill Lane about 1910. These were originally one of Milnthorpe's mills but had become rat-invested slums by the 1890's. At a Public Health enquiry the occupant stated that he often found five dead rats killed by his many cats on the living room floor in the morning. His sick wife slept in the room 'but the cats helped her occupy her time and the rats helped the cats to occupy their time'!

Crosby Lodge Ackenthwaite in 1907 with John and Annie Wilson and their new baby Annie. The house bears Milnthorpe's oldest date stone 1749. One of the chimneys contains a smoking chamber used for curing ham and mutton. 'Baby' Annie later Mrs James Melling and her son Wilson Melling lived here all their lives and both died here.

Harmony Hall is architecturally Milnthorpe's finest house. It was built by a Milnthorpe sea captain Joseph Fayrer who died at Cape Coast Castle in Africa in 1801 while he was dealing in the still legal slave trade.

Fleet House photographed in 1900 when it was the home of a draper Lewis Elburn who had been born in Fleet Street, London, hence the name. The house was dated 1707 but having been Ethel Spry's grocers in the 1940's and 1950's it was demolished in 1966 to make way for a tawdry shack for the District Bank.

Another view of the Blue Row in Church Street around 1900. Note the water butts, cellar flaps for the coal holes and the absence of all traffic on the A6. Some of the houses were half houses consisting of two tiny rooms up and down approached by a lobby shared with the half house next door. There were more 'double' houses higher up the street which had large cellar kitchens staffed by servants.

Ackenthwaite Green House about 1928. This is the family home of the Audlands one of Westmorland's oldest recorded families. For many generations they ran the Ackenthwaite Smithy and William Audland provided iron work for Heversham Church in 1604. In the 1950's the house was extended by Brigadier and Mrs E. G. Audland. After further alterations in 1986 by Sir Christopher and Lady Audland the property received the name of 'The Old House'.

Park Terrace seen here in c.1890 is Milnthorpe's only row of bay windowed houses. They were built around 1875 on the site of some older cottages and featured marble fireplaces, and elaborate plaster work but were roofed in Welsh slate so that allegedly ' they ran like a riddle'.

Ackenthwaite House seen here in pre lawn mower days about 1910 is a larger house dating from around 1800. It also had one of Milnthorpe's first Water Closets in the 1840's. During the 1870's Mrs Isherwood was the tenant 'the wife of the roving Capt. John Nightingale Isherwood, who came home to her from the Antipodes without a moment's warning and always went about carrying a loaded pistol'.

Mallow House (seen from across the grass less 'Green' in May 1908) dates from about 1800 and in the mid nineteenth century was a private school and hydrotherapy nursing home.

The Tattersall Almshouses were built and endowed by William Tattersall a Blackburn brewer who lived at St Anthony's House . They cost £10,000 in 1884 and were to provide a haven for 'those who have once occupied better positions in life but have been reduced through circumstances over which they had no control'.

Before piped water from Lupton Reservoir was 'laid on' in 1906-8 sanitation in the village was appalling and there were several outbreaks of typhoid types of disease. One outbreak nearly killed Doris Mashiter but, happily, she was still telling the tale when she was over 100.

Here we see the watermen resting from pipe laying at Elmsfield.

A relic of past times. Audlands' Pump at The Old House, Ackenthwaite. (right)

Garnett's 'country seat' at Ackenthwaite Farm. In the 1940's this convenience was still used by the farm men as the newly installed bathroom was reserved for the family. (left)

'Maymyo' (almost opposite the Almshouses) photographed from Kirkgate Field as it was nearing completion in 1922. It was built by John Mashiter when he retired from the Post Office and named after the place in Burma where his son Earnest had spent most of the First World War in comparative safety when many other village lads were facing near certain death on The Western Front.

'Maymyo' Town' (which was often miss spelt 'Maymo') as developed next to Mashiters' House. At this time the old name of Church Street was discarded in favour of 'Heversham Road' but the houses did not have numbers only names. Left to Right 'Hillcrest', 'Rosthern', 'Brantholme', 'San Tor', 'Grange View' and 'Malvern'. Until the 1930's these' modern homes' were gas lit but note the wireless aerials.

Kirkgate Field on the western side of Church Street was developed in the late 1920's and the 1930's by Hodgson, Nelson and Scott, a Milnthorpe firm responsible for much building in South Westmorland in the inter-war period.

Here we see 'Overdale' built by Willy Scott. The house incorporated windows and other features re-used from 'The Knoll' a large timber bungalow built by the Miss Harrison's in 1900 but which blew down in c.1922; its site was subsequently occupied by Heversham Vicarage.

The worst type of 'home'. Aerial view of Milnthorpe Workhouse taken in 1966 before the derelict building known latterly as the 'Mental Home' was converted to form Ackenthwaite and Chelsea Courts with other dwellings built in the grounds.

The Workhouse occupying a site on Ackenthwaite Scroggs was designed by Francis Webster in 1815. At the front were the Master's quarters and the Mens' wards. At the back were the workshops, mortuary, privies, nursery and the women!

View of the Workhouse Courtyard
drawn by an indoor pauper in c. 1850.
(below)

The bungalow called 'Dacre' was built by Geoff Scott when he married Sergeant Downing's daughter Dora in 1935. It cost about £600 to build but in 1946 when house prices were at an all time premium Geoff, reputedly, sold it for £3,000. 'Grandma Downing' the sergeant's widow lived next door at ' Ellerdene'. (left)

Crosby House, Ackenthwaite in the process of being built by 'Scotts' for L. G. Powell just before he married Edith Wilson of Crosby Lodge in 1938. (right)

12: Schools

Milnthorpe's brighter and better off boys had been able to go to Heversham Grammar School founded in 1613 by Edward Wilson the ancestor of the Dallam Tower family. But there was no school for poor children until 1819 when the National School began elementary education 'up 40 stairs' in the attic of this house in the Square. (photographed in c.1910).

Being on the coaching route Milnthorpe was a suitable place for small private boarding schools. In 1822 Mrs Hayton opened a boarding and day School at Fir Tree House seen here on the left of the picture of Park Road in c. 1920.

A close up of Miss Mason's School on Harmony Green. Though dating only from 1850 the house is reputed to be haunted. In 1930 Eva Scott recorded that ' the furniture in the room and the crockery on the table were seen to dance a jig of their own volition, accompanied by the banging of doors on a still day'. (below)

MILNTHORPE SCHOOL.

THE Inhabitants of Milnthorpe and Ackenthwaite are informed, that the School erected by MISS MASON will be opened (D. V.) in June, 1851, for the Instruction of Thirty Girls residing in the District of St. Thomas' Church, Milnthorpe, from the ages of Eight to Sixteen.

The Children will receive a religious and plain Education in the usual branches; viz.: Reading, Writing, Cyphering, &c.; also, in Sewing.

The School is intended for the benefit of those Children whose Parents are not able to pay more than Twopence a week, which sum must be paid by each girl on the Monday Morning for the ensuing week. Only one child out of the same family will be admitted on the first opening of the School.

An experienced TEACHER from a good Training School will be appointed, whose Rules must be strictly attended to by the Scholars. A wilful infringement of the Rules of the School will be punished by expulsion.

The girls will be required regularly to attend the Services of the Church, and to wear BONNETS and TIPPETS, which will be provided for them and kept at the School-room.

The School will be under the regular Superintendence of the Rev. R. W. EVANS, the Rev. N. PADWICK, MISS MASON, and Mrs. PADWICK, and will be inspected by occasional Visitors.

All who wish for admittance to the School must apply to the Rev. N. PADWICK, who will give the names to MISS MASON, for her selection.

The Terms and Regulations of the School, also the number of Scholars, may be changed after trial, according to the discretion of the PATRONESS.

March 18th, 1851.

JOHN HUDSON, PRINTER, KENDAL.

Advertisement for Miss Mason's School.

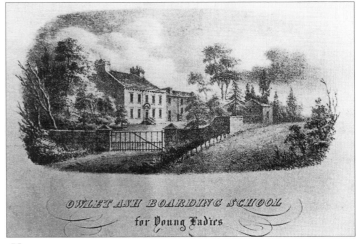

OWLET ASH BOARDING SCHOOL
for Young Ladies

In 1824 Mrs Hayton removed her seminary to Owlett Ash.

The school did not have a playground so the children as seen in this 1930's snap had to make do with the semi bald Green. (below)

St. Thomas School built in 1866 served infants and girls.

Infant's class 1897 (above)

St. Thomas Girls School c.1922 as named by the late Mrs Ladell (Elsie Wilson). (left)

Top Row M. Casson, M. Medcalfe, D. Atkinson. Middle Row D. Hewitt, E. Downing, C. Leather, M. Mashiter, E. Atkinson, E. Parker, M. Wilson, I. Coates.

On chair A. Chamley.

Others on bottom row seated Left to Right E. (Elsie) Wilson, L. Sharples, N. Ellis, D. Downing, N. Sliman, E. Holmes, and J. Clark.

St. Thomas Infant's class of 1949   photographed on the hayfield like Green.

L to R. Back row: Mrs Clark, Brian Barnes, David Bidder, Peter Lacey, Edward Balmer, Malcolm Johnson, Wilson Melling.

Third row Jean Thompson, Betty Balmer, Jean Duncan, Ann Peel, Sheila Garnett, and Ann Biggerdyke.

Second Row Irene Woods, May Peel, Moyra Parsons, Marie Hyde, Pat Benson, Susan Rushton.

Front Row. Raymond Mason, Harvey Gott, Bill Gott, John Metcalf, Robert Metcalfe.

MILNTHORPE NATIONAL SCHOOL.

This School will be re-opened on the 17th July, 1854, and conducted according to the following Rules :—

1. To be under the management of a Committee of the following seven persons, viz. :—

GEORGE E. WILSON, Esq., PATRON.
REV. R. W. EVANS, B. D., VISITOR.
REV. N. PADWICK, M. A., SUPERINTENDANT.
MR. J. HOLME, TREASURER.

MR. M. WHITTAKER.
MR. ISAAC RAWLINSON.
MR. JOSEPH TURNER.

2. Any Child may be admitted being three years of age or upwards, who is recommended by one of the Committee, or a Subscriber of not less than 5s. per annum.

3. Each Child to pay

For Reading	1d. per Week, or 9d. per Quarter.	
For Reading and Writing	2d. „	1s. 6d. „
For Reading, Writing, and Cyphering	3d. „	2s. 3d. „
For every thing taught in the School...	4d. „	3s. 0d. „

If the Child lives out of the township of Heversham with Milnthorpe, to pay one half more.

4. If there are three children of the same parents, to be one-third less than the separate payments would be, provided they pay above one penny a week.

5. Each Child to pay on Monday mornings for the week or quarter in advance. The sum to be entered opposite the Child's name in the Admission Book, and to be paid by the Master to the Treasurer the last Friday in the month.

6. After the Child's name is entered in the Admission Book, to pay half-price during the weeks he is absent from the School, excepting in case of sickness, notice of it having been given to the Master ; before the removal of a Child from School, one week's notice to be given by the Parent to the Master.

7. The School Hours from the first Monday in March to the last Friday in October, to be from nine to twelve, and from half-past one to half-past Four ; at other times from nine to twelve, and one to four.

8. The holidays to be three weeks at Midsummer, and two weeks at Christmas, and every Saturday, Christmas Day, Ash Wednesday, Good Friday, Ascension Day, and Monday and Tuesday in Whitsun week : when there is service on these days the Children are expected to go to Church, as on Sundays.

9. Only such books to be used in the School as are approved of by the Patron, Visitor, and Superintendant : the Children to find their own Bibles and Prayer Books.

10. The School Room to be free for the Bible Society and Church Missionary Meetings ; if wanted for Lectures or Exhibitions, five Shillings to be paid for the use of it towards the School expenses, permission having first been obtained from G. E. Wilson, Esq., or Mr. J. Holme.

11. The Annual Subscriptions to be due the first week in January ; the Book to be presented to the Subscribers by the Master.

J. DAWSON, PRINTER, KENDAL.

Boys School Prospectus of 1854. (left)

In 1834 The Boys National School (seen here about 1900) was opened close to the Bela Clough. The building remained a school until the Primary School was built in 1951. Subsequently its last headmaster Jo Cookson purchased the freehold from the Dallam Estate and converted the school into a house called 'Heronsyke'. (below)

Boy's National School c.1930

Back Row Martin Ashburner, Trevor Coupe, Bill Pearson, Earnie Pearson, Norman Gott, Harvey Gott, Les Richardson, Fred Broomby.

Third Row Ken Shaw, Morris Unsworth, ?, Tom Atkinson, Sandy Atkinson, Bob Todd?, Doug Ashburner. (note the clogs).

Second Row ?, Tom Walker, Frank Sarginson, Ken Watson, Ted Balderstone, Robin Jackson, George Richardson, Ferdie Casson, Charlie Todd.

Front Row Ralph Wilkinson, Tom McGowan, Morris Sliman, Tom Stainton, John Hodgson, Ralph Hodgson.

13: Work

The Bela Comb Mill in 1930 when it was being run by Percy Dobson who later made a fortune partly by obtaining a contract to supply the American forces in Britain with combs. It doesn't sound a big deal until one realises that half a million men wanting to look Brylcream fresh for the girls can use and lose a lot of combs. (below)

Dick Pearson and son bringing horns to the Comb Mill from Sandside Station in c.1910. Before being uncurled and cured the horns were covered in maggots known locally as 'sluffs'. (right)

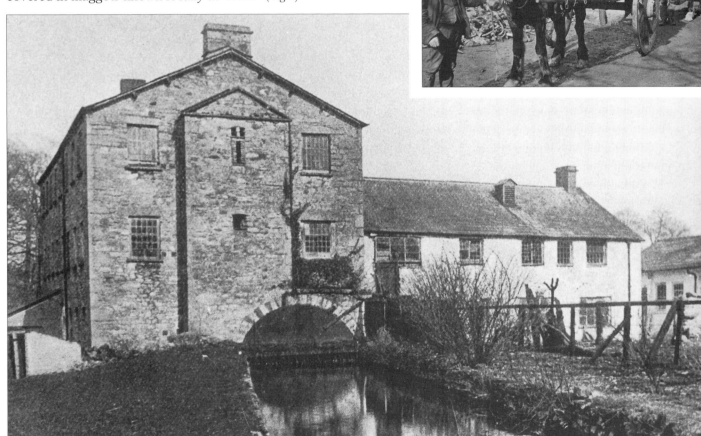

Relics of Milnthorpe's industrial past. The Playing Fields in 1987 showing the former Gas Works House of 1861 on the left. The Corinthians changing room which in c.1780 was part of Potter Fletcher's White paper Mill is in the centre with the Strands Cottages formerly Low Mills on the right.

The Gas Works opened in 1861 and closed in the 1970's. It was the last hand stoked gas works in the country and the last to measure its supply in feet and not in therms. Its plant was taken to Beamish Hall Folk Museum in Durham but still after 30 years it has not yet been put on display.

The Gas works last work force.
L to R. Fred James, John Haykin, Charlie
Shaw.

**Walter Mashiter's Tailors
workshop** in 1905 from an
early 'flash' photograph.
Walter was a Saville Row
trained tailor and his large
staff reflects his flourishing
business. On the extreme
left is a famous village
character Dumby Knowles
and the girl is Walter's niece
Addie.

Post Office presentation on his retirement to Post Man Alf Constable in 1928.

L to R. Norman Knight, Albert Hayes, Mr S. Barr (Post Master), Jack Sliman, Harold Whiteley, Handley Woods, Frank Dunford, Ambrose Birkett. The names of the Post Office officials who are wearing coats are not known.

The Post Officer as rebuilt for John Mashiter in 1897. His brother's tailors shop was next door.

Claughton's Butchers, Main Street, 1900 with G. F. Atkinson the shoemaker holding his hammer and last next door.

The land still provided employment for many villagers as is seen in this photograph of a threshing day believed to be at Ackenthwaite in c.1910. (above)

Ploughing competition 1940's on Ackenthwaite Farm with a steam train on the main line in the background. (below)

Close up of Mr Atkinson standing outside his shop, which was on the other side of the butchers. For some long forgotten reason George Francis was known as 'The Black Admiral'. When not at his last - or in The Cross Keys - he also served as the Parish Clerk and still had time to be a leading Free Mason. (above)

Steam Thresher and mixed gender gang near Milnthorpe c.1910.

A link between the land and urban industry was provided by the American milk canning Firm of Libby McNiel and Libby which opened near Milnthorpe Station in 1934 and employed over 100 workers. The 'ultra modern' red brick buildings ignored all local styles of architecture. The once common silvery coloured milk churns are being unloaded from a lorry underneath the canopy. (right)

Milking for Victory. Libby's war time senior staff.
Left to Right Back Row Reg Benson, Gordon Nelson, Jean Jackson, Walter Williams, Alec McGowan, Harold Hodgson.
Front Row W.A. Moyse, Betty Douthwaite, Wimborne Terry Jenkins (the American manager), Sister M.A. 'Pat' Glover, W.T. Chambers, Vera Webster. (below)

14: Transport

For most of Milnthorpe's history horsepower was the only alternative to foot slogging. Hence blacksmiths were important members of the community.

Here we see Willy Douthwaite shoeing a horse outside The Smithy, Ackenthwaite in 1910. Holding the horse is Tommy Atkinson.

Mashiters Pantechnicon outside Chestnut House, Heversham in 1914.

By the end of the Second World War lorries had ousted horse drawn wagons.

John Ion's lorry is photographed in Haverflatts Lane c.1949. The haulier R.O. Hodgson had his office in the barn in the background which became the site in the 1980's of the Chemists emporium of James E. Rushton Ltd.

The bicycle had revolutionised getting around for most country people by 1900. John Mashiter used his bike daily while he was Post Master between 1890 and 1922 and for recreation. He thought nothing of cycling to Blackpool and back in one day - a round trip of close on a hundred miles. (below)

Thomas Whiteley
Milnthorpe's 'Barber and Umbrella Repairer' on his motor bike c.1910. (left)

District Nurse Helena Bird
on her bike about 1913. She subsequently served in the First World War and was decorated by the King of Serbia and, on her return, was presented with an umbrella by Milnthorpe people. All the other veterans were men: they got a walking stick! (left)

Milnthorpe was served by three railway stations all equally inconveniently situated a mile from the village. Heversham Station on the Furness Railway's Arnside to Hincaster Branch Line was the most attractive though the passenger service never paid. (right)

Perhaps the service was too slow as this 1910 postcard suggests. (below)

OUR LOCAL EXPRESS
Sandside to Kendal and back in one day, via Heversham

90

Heversham got a Royal visitor in Princess Louise who was on her way from Levens Hall to Lowther Castle in 1909.

Milnthorpe Station Inn c1930.

Sandside Station was comparatively large as it was designed to cope with coal deliveries, for limestone freight from the adjacent quarry and also for special excursion trains from Barrow bringing Sunday School trippers and the like to the sands and Haverbrack Common.

The Coronation Scot approaching Milnthorpe Station on the main Line 1937. (below)

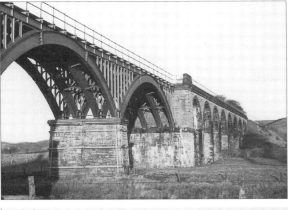

Close up of 'the arches' from the west. (left)

The Furness Railway's Bela Viaduct photographed in c.1877 from the east soon after it was built. The Summer-house on Summerhouse Point can just be seen through the central arches.

93

The branch line passenger service closed in 1940 but was used occasionally by excursion trains. This photograph was taken shortly before the Viaduct was demolished in 1966 a victim of the ' Beeching Axe'.

Around 1900 horse transport was still dominant.

Lady with trap outside The Livery Stables at Ivy House, Main Street in c.1895. (below)

A gentleman sits astride his probably hired horse in The Cross Keys Yard c.1900. (below right)

Motoring was still a novelty and this c.1920 photograph shows that Charabanc trips were popular. Clearly any regulations about over loading are not being observed. (above)

John Fawcett driving one of Milnthorpe's first cars. (left)

Fawcett's Dallam House garage in Milnthorpe Square in 1910. John Fawcett Motor Engineers was founded in 1890 and had as its motto ' as old as and as up to date as the motor industry'. Shortly after the photograph was taken these premises were burnt down in a fire which broke out when many villagers were attending a General Election meeting next door in the Public Rooms. The new buildings which arose on the site are now occupied by Forbouys newsagents.

In 1924 John Fawcett and his sons founded the Dallam Motor Bus

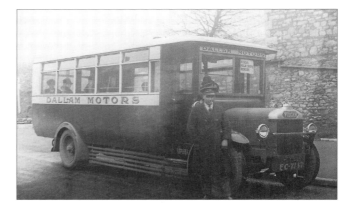

Company whose service eventually connected all South Westmorland villages with Kendal and Lancaster.

Here we see Harry Ryles posing (with fag in mouth) along side his Dallam Bus at the cross roads.

The Fawcett's sold out to Ribble Buses on the 30th November 1950. The next day petrol came off the ration and the era of private car travel for all began.

On their last day buses and staff lined up in the Square for a farewell photograph. *L to R.* Buses. Bedford of 1941, the 'Old Lion' 1928, Seddon 1947, Leyland Lion 1932, Leyland Cheta 1939, Leyland Lion 1937, Leyland Lion 1935, Seddon 1948.

L to R Staff. Fred Strong, Harry Ryles, Olga Denny, Doris Hyde, Jo Walsh, Jack Black, Des Palmer, John Walls, Cliff Thomas, Donnie Holden, Ronnie Mattock, Harold Fawcett, Jack Fawcett.

As the photos of traffic free streets indicate private cars were still rare in the 1930's. Even so some fine motors were seen around the village. Dr. J.R. Caldwell of Stoneleigh is seen here on the right with his Lagonda in 1937. On the left George Nicholson with the Doctor's Standard SS-JM 751 in 1935.

15: War

The first half of the twentieth century was marred by war. But for Milnthorpe the terrible era began triumphantly when an arch was erected at the entrance to Main Street to welcome local volunteers returning from the Boer War. They marched from Sandside Station to the church steps where they were given gold watches.

The Volunteer Corps soon re-christened the Territorial Army was popular amongst village lads partly because they got a holiday in camp each summer. Here a local posse lines up behind Sergeant Willy Scott who is slouching on the grass.

The 1907 funeral procession of Volunteer part time soldier Henry Abbatt crossing the Green. In the background is Stoneleigh then the home of Dr. Seagrave. The larger of the two cottages next door contained the sweet shop of 'Toffee Johnny' Gray who hanged himself in the back yard shed following the visit of police officers from Liverpool who were investigating a murder. The cottages (but not the shed) were demolished by Dr. Fuller in c.1920 - to enlarge Stoneleigh's garden.

Real War began in 1914. Here are the 'first to go' many of whom were 'to be lost'.

Back Row Mennel Rheam, Ralph Thompson, Edward Ashburner, and Enos Dixon, Edward C. Mashiter, Thomas Coward, Herbert Thompson.

Second Row William Knight, Jack Wilkinson, Fred Wilkinson, Robert Hudson, Charlie Wilson, Ernest Mashiter.

Front Row Charlie Hyde, Jack Woof, ?, Jim Garth, Tommy Wilson, William Towers?.

Fireman Carter's Imperial War Graves tombstone in Milnthorpe Cemetery. He was killed when he fell - or was he pushed or trying to escape - from a troop train near Milnthorpe Station. Although there were hundreds of soldiers and sailors on the train 'no one saw anything' and the only witness was, of all people, a 'Chinaman who could not speak English'; no one at the inquest could speak Chinese. (left)

A Highland Regiment leaving Milnthorpe Station en route for a training camp at Farleton in 1912. (below)

Troops at Milnthorpe Station in 1916 apparently bound for The Western Front. (above)

The names of Volunteers were recorded on a Roll of Honour placed on the wall of St. Thomas' School. It is now preserved in the Church. (left)

Great excitement was caused in 1915 when a Royal Flying Corps airship came down at Moss End. As late as 1977 this photo could not be published in the 'Our Village' booklet because it still came under the Official Secrets Act.

Milnthorpe 'lost' 21 young men from a population of less than a thousand. Their names were inscribed on a wooden cross (donated by Colonel Weston MP) seen here when set up in the church yard and as decorated for the Church's 150 Anniversary in 1987.

A grander War Memorial costing nearly £3,000 was erected on the Green in 1920. (left)

Peace Celebrations June 1919. Renee Casson is Britannia whilst a pouting Elsie Atkinson (later Mrs Bragg) walks alongside the float. Elsie was cross because she had been asked to carry Handley Woods' pipe down to the Playing Field ' and it was hot and burnt her hand'. (below)

'Sara the Land Girl who came from Manchester' feeding turkeys at Overthwaite c.1945. At a time when meat was rationed at 4 shillings per person per week a turkey for Christmas was an undreamed of luxury for most people as they cost £5 'at the back door' (the rural equivalent of 'under the counter') compared to £1-30 shillings for a goose.

During the Second World War conflict actually touched Milnthorpe as bombs were dropped on Slackhead and Overthwaite within a mile or two of the village. The Overthwaite bomb of 1942 caused the deepest crater. (above)

Perhaps for security reasons there are few photographs of the Home Guard. This blurred snap was taken on the Green at the 'stand down' parade 1st. December 1944. Curiously most members of Milnthorpe's Dads' Army came from Burton and Holme. (below left)

The same parade showing the buildings on the south side of the Green. Left to Right The Cookery Rooms used for Senior Girls Domestic lessons, Cowards' Shoemakers, Moss' Lodging House at the Sun Tavern, Harold Whiteley's Barbers at The Tavern Loft and Fountain House the home of the Ormerod family. (below)

Bela Prisoner of War Camp.

In 1942/3 a Prisoner of War Camp for Italians was established on the banks of the river Bela at Hang Bridge. Later they were joined at 'The Camp' by Germans who were not officially repatriated until 1947. Afterwards many stayed on at Bela River as farm workers. Even during the war when 'fraternisation' was not allowed there were easy relations between prisoners and the local population and it was claimed that the camp's barbed wire fences were really needed to keep the camp followers out rather than the prisoners in! After the war several POW's married local girls.

B/20012 POW Josef Otto Bina on his bike at The Camp. Jo married Joan Spedding from Milnthorpe.

The Bela River dance band on a visit to nearby Holme in 1947. (above)

Docket for camp currency. (right)

106

Teach your self English magazine for POW's. (below)

An attempt at a 'Merry Christmas' but with Teutonic emphasis on education! (right)

English for All

No. 43   Fortnightly for Germans   16th December, 1947

A Merry Christmas 1947

RECIPE FOR AN ENGLISH CHRISTMAS PUDDING
(Post-War Austerity)[12]

¼ lb. breadcrumbs	½ lb. dried fruit
¼ lb. flour	1 dried egg (egg powder)
¼ lb. suet	2 tablespoonsful of treacle[13]
½ lb. brown sugar	1 teacupful of milk

Method: 1. Mix all dry ingredients.
2. Add egg-powder, treacle and milk.
3. Beat the mixture well.
4. Boil for 6 hours.

It is customary to put a lucky[14] sixpence into the pudding mixture. Sometimes in pre-war days small silver charms[15] were added, a tiny thimble,[16] a horseshoe, a bell and others. Whoever found one of them in his piece of pudding could expect some good luck in the coming months.

The Christmas pudding is always decorated with holly and before it is brought in brandy is poured over it and set alight so that the pudding is surrounded by blue flames. This does not only improve the taste of the pudding, but it is also one of the many symbols of Light triumphing over darkness at the time of the winter solstice.[17]

1. moist—*feucht*; 2. shredded suet—*geschabtes Nierenfett*; 3. currants—*Korinthen*; 4. mixed peel—*kandierte Pomeranzen—und Apfelsinenschalen*; 5. breadcrumbs—

Milnthorpe had its share of war heroes. Gordon Audland C.B.E. became a Brigadier General, Sid Tugman and Eddie Rushton went ashore on D Day, Squadron Leader Richard Miles won the DFC, John 'Ponny' Balmer won the B.E.M. for rescuing an airman from a burning plane and Dr. Ken Bingham was photographed by Cecil Beaton doing pioneering work with penicillin in North Africa. In his memoirs Beaton wrote ' Major Bingham with his bright eyes, looked little more than a schoolboy' - but Binghams were never tall!

Sq. Ld. Richard Miles winning the D. F. C. Sadly Richard was later killed in a flying accident in Canada while on active service. (above)

Major Ken Bingham M.C. (left)

Ponny Balmer outside Buckingham Palace with his wife and sister after receiving the B.E.M. from GeorgeVI -' who was very nice but wore make up'. (right)

VE Day 8th May 1945. Willy Scott has just hoisted his Union Jack and is admiring his 'Dig For Victory' tattie patch, which throughout the war replaced his front lawn at 'Mylngarth', Church Street.

Fancy Dress Parade in The Square Victory Day 8th June 1946.
Fashions had changed during the war so that amongst the ladies only Sheila Wheatman on the right in the parade is wearing a fetching hat. But Willy Douthwaite in the crowd at the left sports a pre-war homburg.

16: Fun

Royal occasions have always been celebrated fully in Milnthorpe as is shown in this 1902 photograph of Coronation Day cycle parade gathering on The Green.

Milnthorpe's beacon on Haverbrack being made for the Coronation of George V in 1911. Sir Maurice Bromley -Wilson's agent L. Nanson informed the authorities that it was 35 feet high, on a site 359 feet above sea level and that nine other fires could be seen. (left)

The village lads used the roof of the newly erected public lavatories as their vantage point for the Silver Jubilee celebrations in 1935. (below)

Our Calico Ball at Milnthorpe,
April 22nd, 1908

Invitation to a fancy dress ball in the Public Rooms.

This snap taken during the festivities for the Silver Jubilee of King George V and Queen Mary in 1935 shows Leslie Powell in floppy hat and the village bell-man Arthur Ashburner holding his bell. (right)

112

The crowded revellers at the Fancy Dress Ball. The hall floor was highly polished and sprung, and was regarded as the best in the district - "including the Kendal Town Hall". Sadly it was ruined when the tip-up seats were screwed onto its parquet when the Public Rooms served as a makeshift cinema in the 1940s and 1950s.

113

For outdoor events everything
depended on the weather.
Dallam Tower Sports 1912.

Chapel trip in the rain c.1928.

The main leisure activity   dependant on the weather is the most popular - gardening.

1948 seems to have been a good year judging by the display of produce at the Milnthorpe Allotments Associations' eighth Show held in the Memorial Hall - formerly the Public Rooms.

The Milnthorpe Silver Band   photographed outside the old Bull's Head about 1910.

   Chris Scott wearing his T.A. uniform sits in the middle. Officially Chris was said to have been 'killed' at the Dardanelles in 1915 but there were subsequent rumours that he had survived and 'escaped' on a hospital ship for Australia.

Sergeant Park's One Man Band. He was Milnthorpe's 'Bobby' from 1906-20.

Milnthorpe Mouth Organ Band 1937.
L to R Back Row Ken Adamson, Fred Broomby, ?, Ernie Pearson, Jack Warne, Harry Murray, Doug Ashburner, Maurice Pearson, ?, George Webb.
Front Tom Jones, ?, George Wilson, Jack Adamson, Ted Lacy, Bert Wilson.

Photo   Savoy Studio.

TEDDY DAVENPORT
AND HIS
REVELLERS' BAND,

the most popular combination playing in the County.   Rhythm
and Syncopation is what is wanted, and the Revellers' have it.
Secretaries kindly book their dates as early as possible as the Band
are heavily booked ahead.

For Terms, Photograph, vacant dates, apply :—
E. DAVENPORT, Rigny Bank, Milnthorpe.

Teddy Davenport with his Band. C.1935 He 'could make a piano play by itself'. (left & right)

Milnthorpe Girl Guides 1950.

Back Row L to R. Irene Fawcett, Mrs Corless, Nora Watts.

Middle Row Norma Taylor, Myra Davenport, Melita Ashburner, Daphne Hyde, Ruth Davenport.

Front Row Brenda Walsh, Mary Blenkharn, Pat Cooper, Irene Gott, Valerie Cairns. (below)

The Milnthorpe Wrestling Academy c.1910. Mr Hodgson landlord of the Cross Keys presides over the trophy table at a prize giving ceremony in the Public Rooms.

Cricket has a long history in Milnthorpe as G.E. Wilson of Dallam Tower was a keen supporter of the game and was President of Kendal Cricket Club in the 1850's. But there are no records or old photographs of a Milnthorpe Club before c.1890.

This 1925 photo of a 'six a side team?' might have been taken in the Beetham Road Cricket Field as the wall in the background seems to be that of the garden of Bela View. In front of the striped pavilion are: (right)

left to Right Back Row: Harold Wilkinson, Geoff Scott, and Geoff Morton.

Front Row: Willy Scott, Jimmy Wilkinson, and Tommy Greenhow.

Milnthorpe footballers 1910 in The Town Field behind Church Street.

Milnthorpe Corinthians 1937-1938 outside The Coach and Horses.

Back Row L to R Joe Battersby, J. Jackson, J. Fishwick, W. Houghton, P. Dobson, J. Wilkinson, J.Myer, Fred Gothard, R. Sumpton.

Second Row. J. Robinson, C. Rooke, Ted Lacey, Harry (Midge) Shaw, Sid Tugman, Tom Shaw, H. Nicholson, Fred Shaw, Norman Arkwright.

Front Row. Harry Newhouse, Bill Shaw, Fred Parker, T. Nicholson, B. Armer, F. Moorby, John Garnett.

Sitting on the ground. Doug Ashburner, C. Sumpton, Dick (Slip) Garth.

122

Milnthorpe Amateur Dramatic Society was founded in 1900 and flourished until c.1965. Here we see the caste of ' The Shaugron' in 1920. They have taken their back cloth out into the old Bull's Head yard for the photo. Note the cobbles.

L to R. Billy ?, L. Wilson, J. Wilkinson, Will Garnett, Harold Hyde, J. Wilkinson, ?, ?, J.K. Jackson,

Sitting ?, Marjorie Bateman, Mrs Halliwell, Mr. Halliwell, Freda Walker, Alice Clark.

'Hay Fever' 1946.

L to R. Betty Douthwaite, Gatewood Whittaker, Vera Webster, Basil Morley, Ann Dighton, John Glover, Patrick Byrne, ?, Cora Dawson.

Milnthorpe Amateurs in 'The Gleam' 1948.

Left to right: Phyllis Bingham, Zulieka Ireland, Vera Webster, Ferdie Casson, Kenneth Jackson and Edith Crossley.

'The Gleam' was a modernistic and historically important play set in a doctor's house at the inception of the National Health Service which was currently being introduced.

It was after this production that a section of the company split off from the Milnthorpe Amateurs to form the South Westmorland Stage and Screen Society. The ostensible reason for the split was the reluctance of the Milnthorpe old stagers to change producers for each play, and to widen the repertoire from the traditional farces, light comedies and thrillers to more demanding and adventurous pieces. An underlying reason was the age old mutual suspicion between native villagers and 'off comers who wanted to take over the whole show'. The 'new' SWSSS still flourishes but the Amateurs disbanded in the 1960's.

Sat. Feb. 18.

Stupendous Paramount Attraction
Gary Cooper with George Raft and
Frances Dee in
SOULS AT SEA
A Thrilling Drama of the Slave Trade.

Thurs. & Fri. Feb. 23 & 24.

The Biggest British Comedy Success
of all time
THE CRAZY GANG
(Flanagan & Allen, Naughton & Gold,
and Nervo & Knox) in
"ALF'S BUTTON AFLOAT"
You must not miss this—Book now.

Sat. Feb. 25.

The Paramount Epic of Pioneer Days
Joel McCrea, Bob Burns, Frances Dee
and a cast of thousands, in
"WELLS FARGO"
This film takes nearly two hours to show
so please be in your seat early.

THE
CINEMA
MILNTHORPE

PROGRAMME
For FEBRUARY 1939.
Subject to alteration without notice.

Times—Saturdays & Bank Holidays
2-30, 6-30, 8-45.
Other Nights—7-15
ADMISSION
1/3, 9d. 6d.
MATINEES— 3d. & 6d.
Children with Adults, HALF PRICE
except Saturdays & Bank Holidays.

Seats reserved & not paid for will not
be guaranteed after advertised time of
commencement.
Ample Car Parking Facilities within
20 yards of Cinema.

Thurs. & Fri. Feb. 2 & 3.

Will Hay with Graham Moffat and
Moore Marriott in
"CONVICT 99"
An outstanding British Comedy.

Sat. Feb. 4.

Pat O'Brien, Wayne Morris and
George Brent in
"SUBMARINE D.1."
A thrilling drama of the American Navy
with wonderful scenes of rescue from a
sunken submarine.

Thurs. & Fri. Feb. 9 & 10.

Emlyn Williams, Hugh Williams and
Lesley Brook in
"Dead Men Tell No Tales"
A thrilling all British Crime Drama
from the novel "Norwich Victims"
by Francis Beeding.

Programme for 'the CINEMA Milnthorpe'.

From the 1920's to the 1960's 'the Pictures' were shown in The Public Rooms later called The Memorial Hall. Even in the 1940's and 1950's when the hall was decked out with rickety plush seats, culled from a blitzed cinema in Salford. The attraction was about as sleazy a flea pit as any in the land. For the intermittent performances the screen was hung over the entrance and the normal seating arrangements turned round so the hall's stage served as the balcony. Ice cream was available but many of the patrons chose to bring in fish and chips for refreshments.

Sat. Feb. 11.

John Howard, Reg. Denny, J. Barrymore
— in —
BULLDOG DRUMMOND
COMES BACK

Also another of Clarence E. Mulford's
Western Dramas
"HOPALONG RIDES ALONE"

Tues. Feb. 14.

The one and only MAE WEST in
Every Day's a Holiday

You simply must take this opportunity
and see this famous Star.

Thurs. & Fri. Feb. 16 & 17.

Smashing BRITISH Success
TOM WALLS
with Renee Saint-Cyr and star cast in

"STRANGE BOARDERS"

One of the Public Rooms most popular events was the Annual Show of the Milnthorpe Fur and Feather Fanciers. Unfortunately no pictures have come to light of this show though here we see one of the regular exhibitors **Willy Douthwaite** with his prize winning poultry photographed at Ackenthwaite in 1930.

And finally Milnthorpe Women's Institute   Children's production of Cinderella 1947.

Back Row L to R: Tony Wood, William Hird, Sally Outhwaite, Brenda Walsh, David Hyde?, Colin Gott, Dulcie Williams, Brian Broomfield

Middle Row: Peter Kirby, Neil Scott, Marie Hyde, Janet Miles, Pamela Bingham, Joan Fothergill, Irene Woods, Judith Mason, John Williams, Mavis Gott, Margaret Warne, Jean Duncan, Ann Fishwick, Mary Fishwick., and Daphne Hyde.

Seated: Malcolm Walsh, Roger Bingham, Russell Holmes, Frank Fothergill, Christopher Thompson, Hugh Miles, Micky Kirby.

Printed by St Edmundsbury Press, Bury St Edmunds, IP33 3TU